Newmarket Public Library

P9-ARJ-312

FUN
TO LEARN
SPANISH

COMPILED BY JOHN GRISEWOOD
ILLUSTRATED BY KATY SLEIGHT

KING*f*isher

NEW YORK

JUN 1 2 2001

KINGFISHER
Larousse Kingfisher Chambers Inc.
95 Madison Avenue
New York, New York 10016

First published in 2000

10 9 8 7 6 5 4 3 2 1

Copyright © Kingfisher Publications Plc 1991

All rights reserved under International and
Pan-American Copyright Conventions.

ISBN 0-7534-5302-9

Translator: Keltse Iriondo
Cover design: The Pinpoint Design Company
Illustrations: Katy Sleight

Phototypeset by Wyvern Typesetting, Bristol.
Printed in Spain

About your book

All the Spanish words are printed in bold, heavy type like this—**el sombrero**; the English words are printed in ordinary type like this—hat.

In Spanish *all* nouns are either masculine or feminine—not just obvious ones such as "girl" (**una niña**) or "man" (**un hombre**), but every word. So "snow" (**la nieve**) is feminine, but "sun" (**el sol**) is masculine. That is why most of the nouns in this book have **el** or **la** (the) or **un** or **una** (a or an) before them. **El** shows that the word is masculine—**el libro** (the book)—and **la** shows the word is feminine—**la casa** (the house). Before a word in the plural, **el** and **la** become **los** and **las**—**los libros** for "the books" and **las sillas** for "the chairs."

When learning Spanish words by heart, it is important to learn them with the **el** or **la** that goes before. It will make learning the language much easier.

Upside-down questions
You will notice that there are upside-down question marks (¿) before question sentences in Spanish. This is not a mistake. This sign is used before all questions in Spanish.

How to say the words
We have deliberately not shown how the words are pronounced. There are sounds in Spanish that are very different from any we make in English. So it is better to ask a teacher or someone who speaks the language how to pronounce the words correctly.

When to use *tu*
Tu is used for "you" in Spanish when speaking to a close friend or a relative. In all other cases use **usted** for one person and **ustedes** if there is more than one person.

The publishers would like to thank Universal Translators of London for their help in checking the translation of this book.

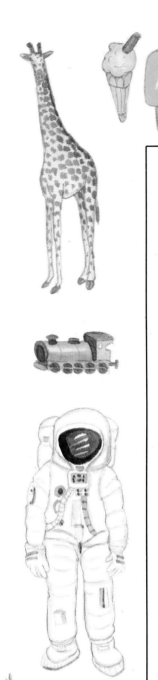

Contents   Contenido

shoulder
el hombro

toe
**el dedo
del pie**

teeth
los dientes

neck
el cuello

chest
el pecho

chin
la barbilla

finger
el dedo

The body
El cuerpo

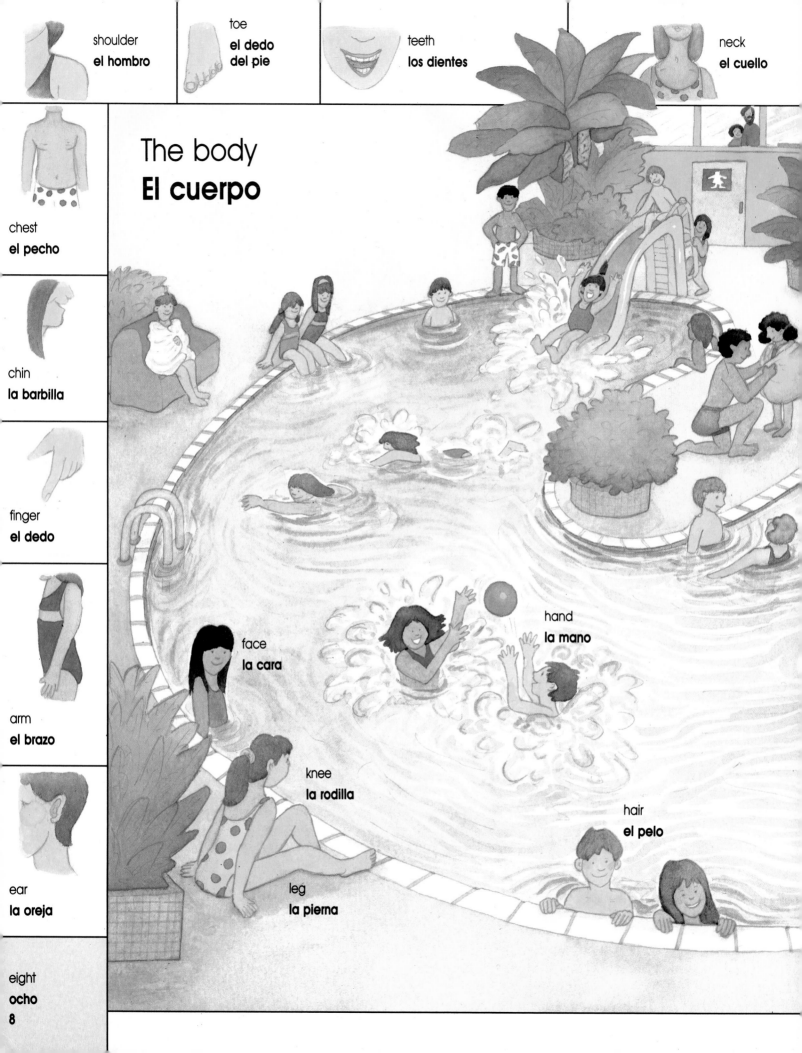

arm
el brazo

face
la cara

hand
la mano

knee
la rodilla

hair
el pelo

ear
la oreja

leg
la pierna

eight
ocho

8

ankle **el tobillo**

thumb **el pulgar**

nose **la nariz**

eye **el ojo**

mouth **la boca**

stomach **el estómago**

bottom **el trasero**

swimming pool **la piscina**

elbow **el codo**

head **la cabeza**

back **la espalda**

tongue **la lengua**

beard **la barba**

whistle **un silbato**

foot **el pie**

cheek **la mejilla**

nine **nueve**

9

swing
el columpio

shower
la regadera

window
la ventana

clock
el reloj

rug
el tapete

bed
una cama

pitchfork
la horca

shovel
la pala

bathtub
la tina

The house
La casa

chimney
la chimenea

roof
el techo

tree
el árbol

trunk
el tronco

wall
la pared

bush
el arbusto

bathroom
el baño

kitchen
la cocina

floor
el suelo

path
el camino

backyard
el jardín

flowerbed
un macizo

greenhouse
un invernadero

lawn
el césped

ten
diez
10

table
la mesa

chair
la silla

stove
la estufa

television
la televisión

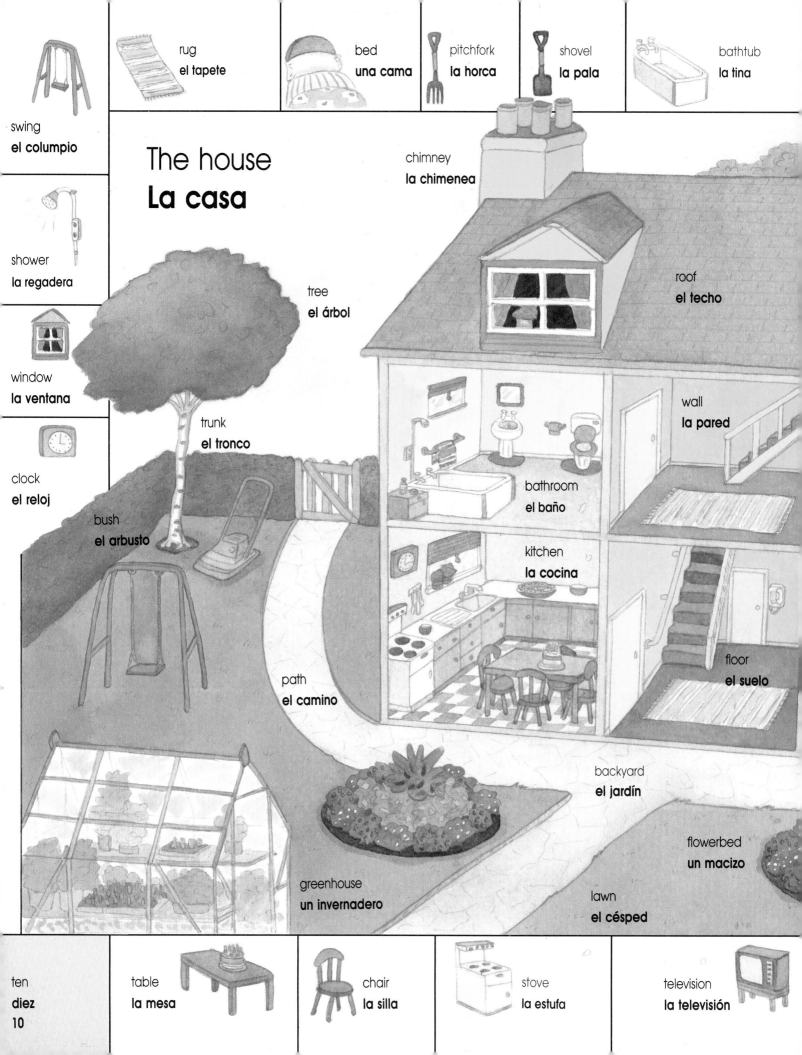

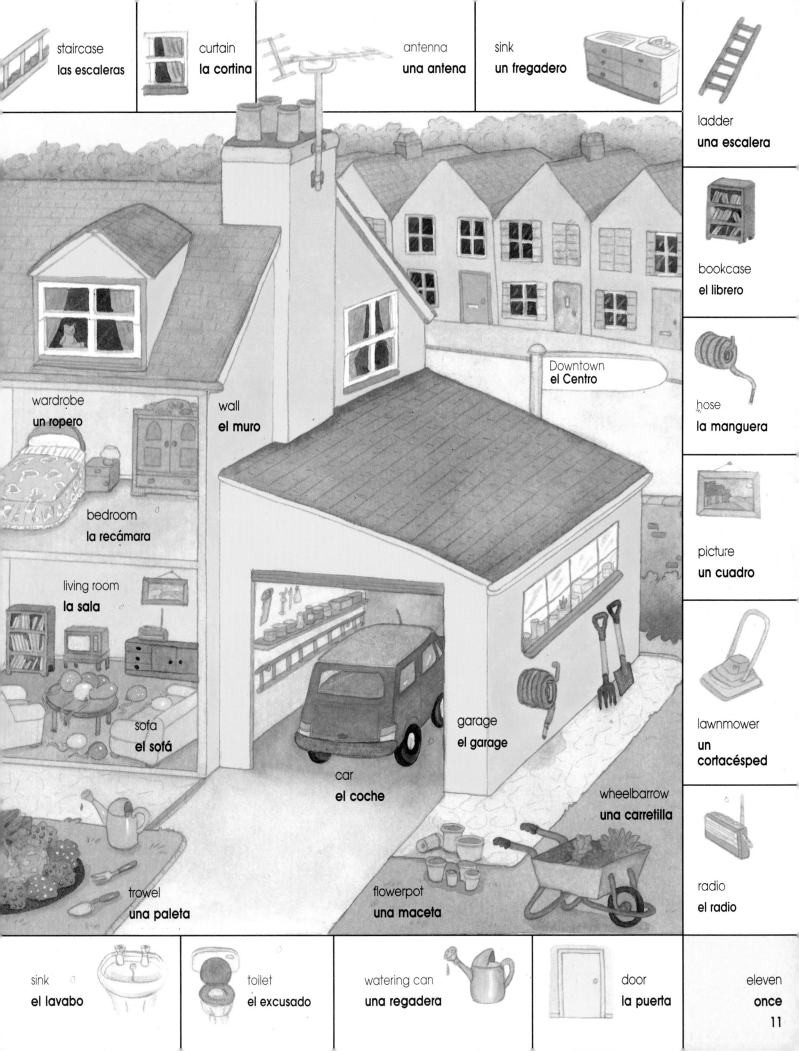

staircase
las escaleras

curtain
la cortina

antenna
una antena

sink
un fregadero

ladder
una escalera

bookcase
el librero

hose
la manguera

picture
un cuadro

lawnmower
un cortacésped

radio
el radio

wardrobe
un ropero

wall
el muro

Downtown
el Centro

bedroom
la recámara

living room
la sala

sofa
el sofá

garage
el garage

car
el coche

wheelbarrow
una carretilla

trowel
una paleta

flowerpot
una maceta

sink
el lavabo

toilet
el excusado

watering can
una regadera

door
la puerta

eleven
once

11

belt
el cinturón

hairbrush
el cepillo para el pelo

socks
los calcetines

tights
las mallas

handkerchief
el pañuelo

comb
el peine

umbrella
el paraguas

skirt
la falda

undershirt
la camiseta

What shall we wear?
¿Qué nos pondremos?

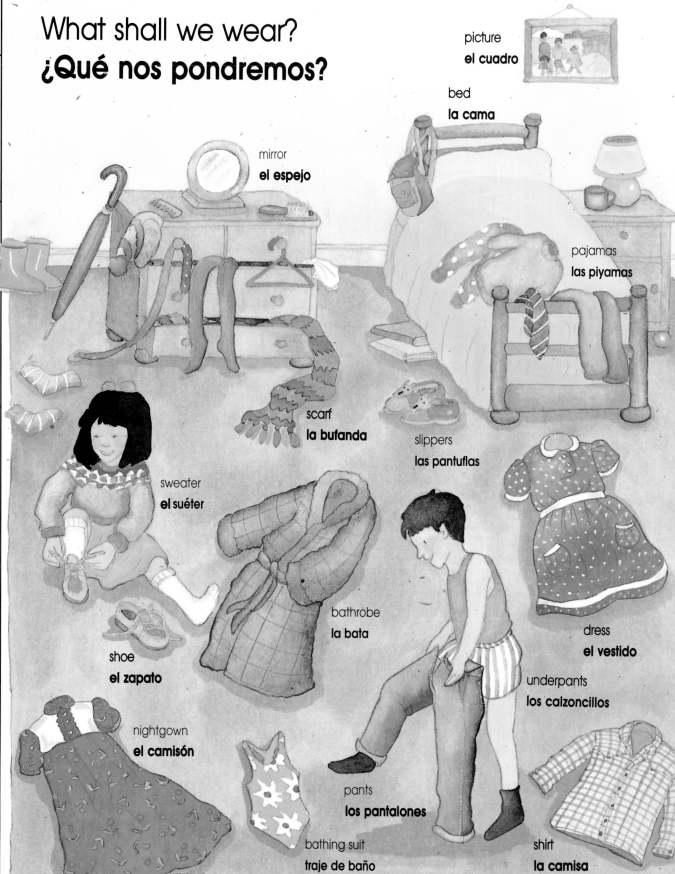

picture
el cuadro

bed
la cama

mirror
el espejo

pajamas
las piyamas

scarf
la bufanda

slippers
las pantuflas

sweater
el suéter

bathrobe
la bata

dress
el vestido

shoe
el zapato

underpants
los calzoncillos

nightgown
el camisón

pants
los pantalones

bathing suit
traje de baño

shirt
la camisa

tie
la corbata

hanger
el gancho

backpack
la mochila

pocket
el bolsillo

helmet
el casco

astronaut
el astronauta

firefighter
el bombero

ballet dancer
la bailarina

knight
el caballero

cape
la capa

dog collar
el collar

leash
la corréa

mittens
los mitones

gloves
los guantes

raincoat
el impermeable

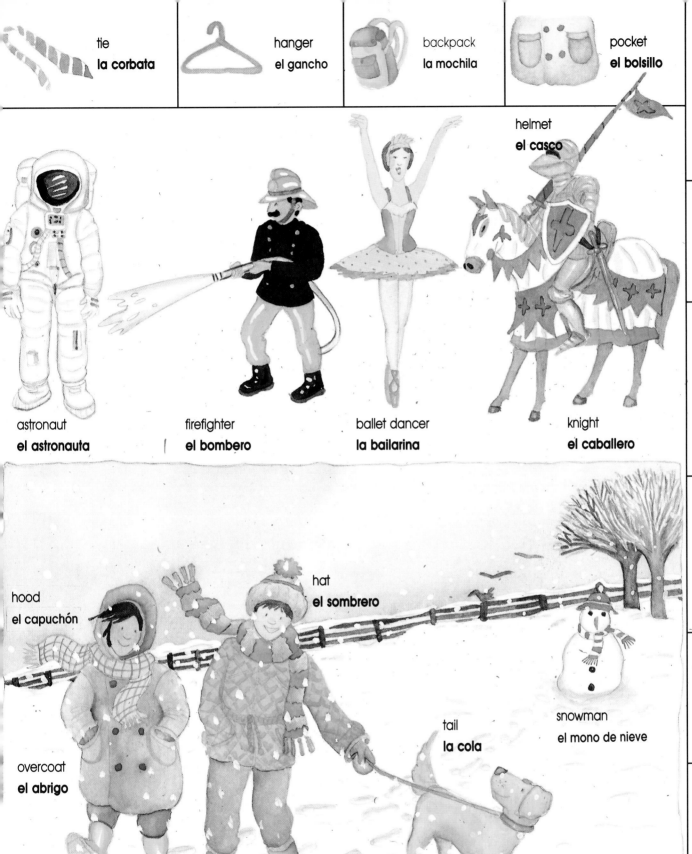

hood
el capuchón

hat
el sombrero

overcoat
el abrigo

tail
la cola

snowman
el mono de nieve

rubber boots
las botas de hule

thirteen
trece

13

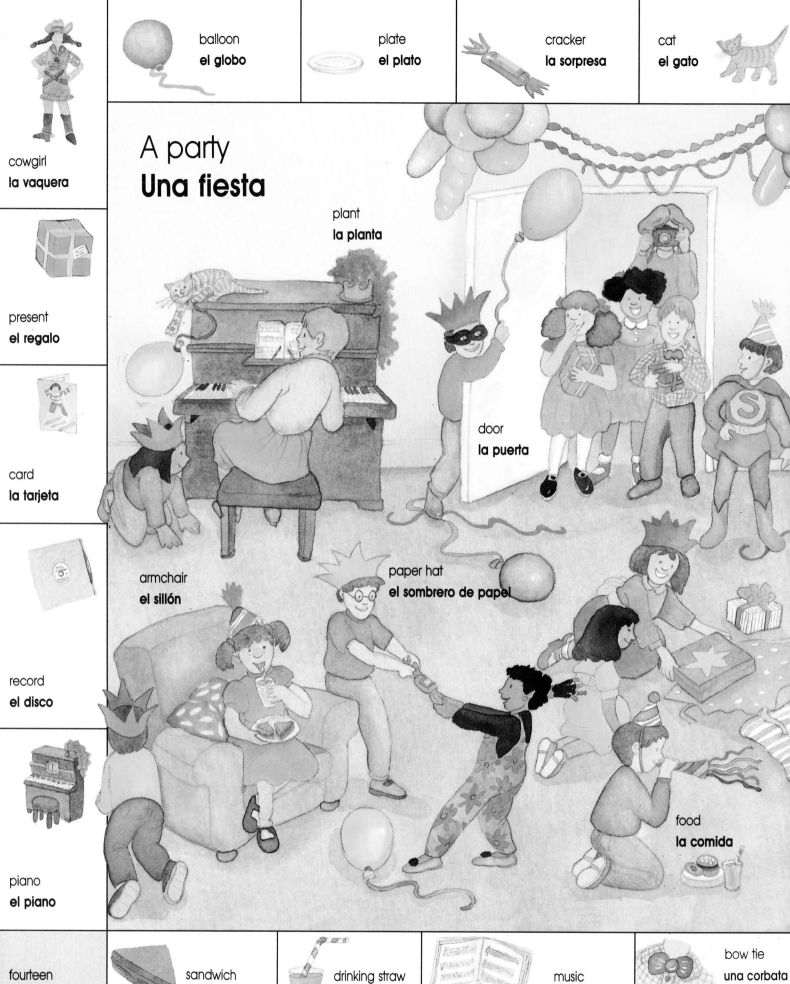

cowgirl
la vaquera

present
el regalo

card
la tarjeta

record
el disco

piano
el piano

balloon
el globo

plate
el plato

cracker
la sorpresa

cat
el gato

A party
Una fiesta

plant
la planta

door
la puerta

armchair
el sillón

paper hat
el sombrero de papel

food
la comida

fourteen
catorce
14

sandwich
el sandwich

drinking straw
el popote

music
la música

bow tie
una corbata de moño

| mask
la máscara | bottle
la botella | lantern
la linterna | lollipop
la paleta |

cake
el pastel

shelf
el estante

gelatin
la gelatina

glass
el vaso

dog
el perro

blindfold
la pañoleta

puppy
el cachorro

clown
el payaso

hamburger
la hamburguesa

glass
el vaso

cookie
la galleta

potato chip
las papitas fritas

candle
la vela

camera
la cámara

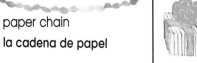
paper chain
la cadena de papel

 bow
el moño

 spoon
la cuchara

 record player
el tocadiscos

fifteen
quince

flashlight
la linterna

domino
el dominó

bunk
la litera

puppet
el títere

Playtime
El recreo

shelves
los estantes

painting
la pintura

book
el libro

scarf
la bufanda

toy chest
la caja de juguetes

soldier
el soldado

sailor
el marinero

boy
el niño

tricycle
el triciclo

kite
la cometa

bookbag
la mochila

sixteen
dieciséis

16

Noah's ark
el arca de Noé

spinning top
el trompo

paints
las pinturas

railroad track
la vía del tren

locomotive
la locomotora

airplane
el avión

blocks
los cubos

dollhouse
la casita de muñecas

teddy bear
el osito de peluche

ladder
la escalera

comforter
la colchoneta

girl
la niña

bridge
el puente

easel
el caballete

mobile
el móvil

jump rope
la cuerda para saltar

soccer ball
el balón de fútbol

roller skates
los patines de ruedas

jigsaw puzzle
el rompecabezas

seventeen
diecisiete

17

dolphin
un delfín

fish
un pez

monkev
un chango

spider
una araña

parrot
un perico

penguin
un pinguïno

butterfly
una mariposa

tiger
un tigre

Noah's Ark
El Arca de Noé

two eagles
dos águilas

two elephants
dos elefantes

two camels
dos camellos

eighteen
dieciocho
18

wolf
un lobo

porcupine
un puercoespín

leopard
un leopardo

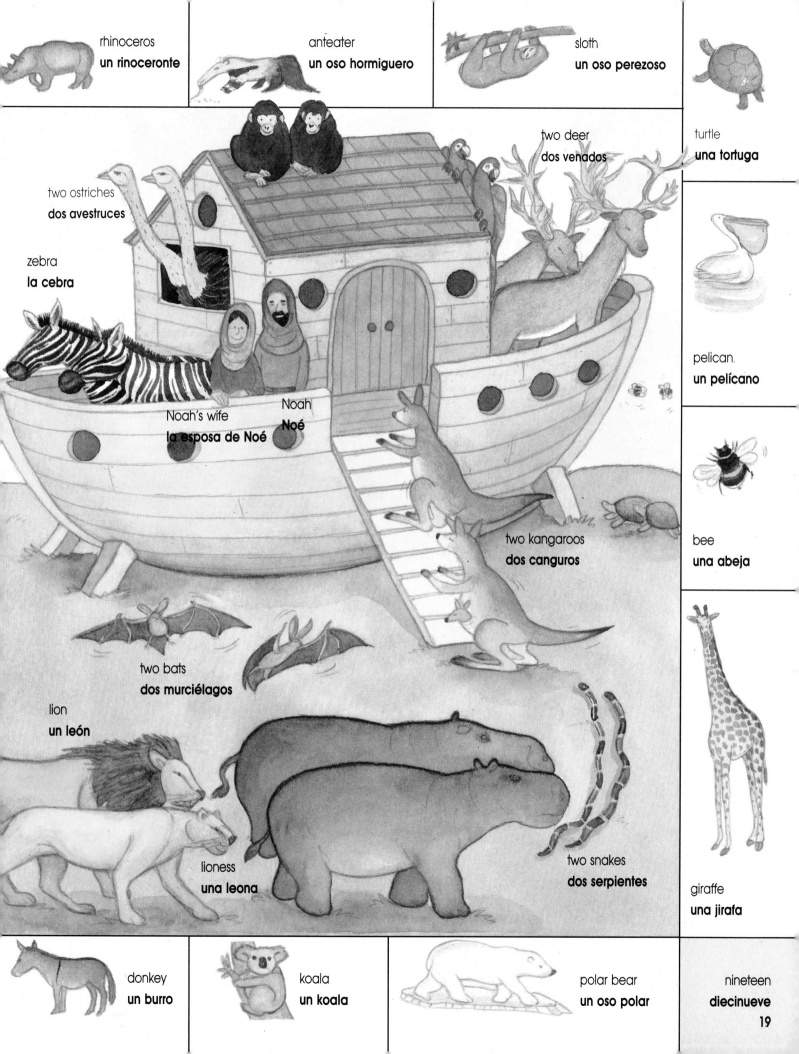

rhinoceros
un rinoceronte

anteater
un oso hormiguero

sloth
un oso perezoso

turtle
una tortuga

two deer
dos venados

two ostriches
dos avestruces

zebra
la cebra

pelican.
un pelícano

Noah's wife
la esposa de Noé

Noah
Noé

two kangaroos
dos canguros

bee
una abeja

two bats
dos murciélagos

lion
un león

giraffe
una jirafa

lioness
una leona

two snakes
dos serpientes

donkey
un burro

koala
un koala

polar bear
un oso polar

nineteen
diecinueve

19

barge
una barcaza

tent
una tienda de campaña

trailer
un trailer

hood
el cofre

canoe
una canoa

hemlet
el casco

wheel
una rueda

helicopter
el helicóptero

twenty
veinte
20

On the move
En camino

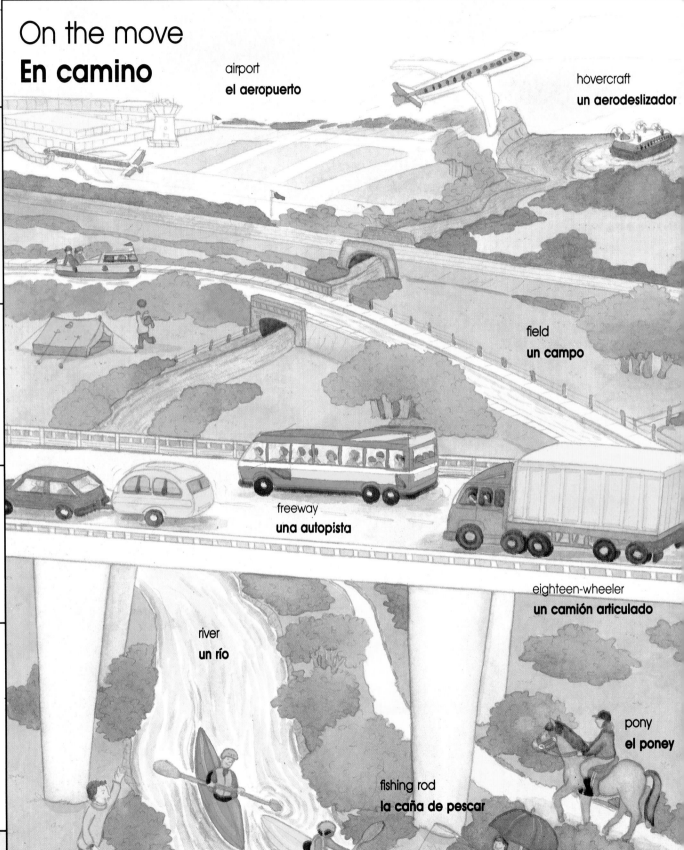

airport
el aeropuerto

hovercraft
un aerodeslizador

field
un campo

freeway
una autopista

eighteen-wheeler
un camión articulado

river
un río

pony
el poney

fishing rod
la caña de pescar

paddle
un remo

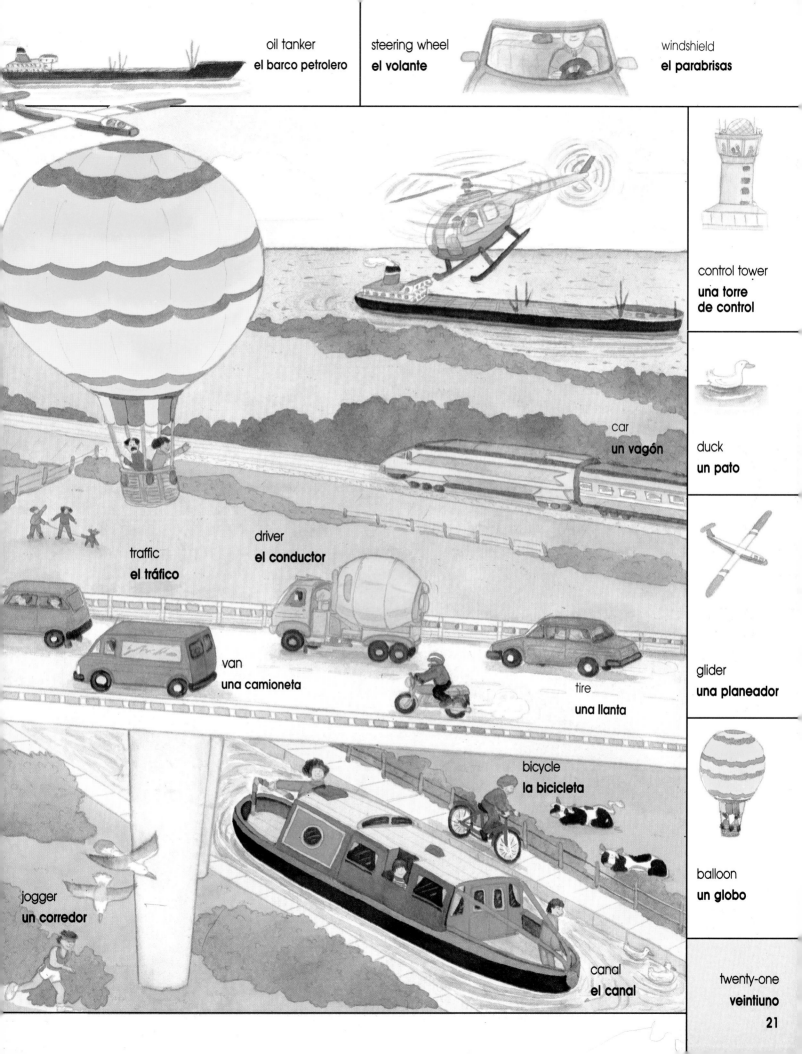

oil tanker
el barco petrolero

steering wheel
el volante

windshield
el parabrisas

control tower
una torre de control

duck
un pato

glider
una planeador

balloon
un globo

car
un vagón

driver
el conductor

traffic
el tráfico

van
una camioneta

tire
una llanta

bicycle
la bicicleta

jogger
un corredor

canal
el canal

newsseller
**un vendedor
de periódicos**

factory
la fábrica

truck
el camión

bridge
el puente

The town
La ciudad

airport
el aeropuerto

grass
el pasto

field
el campo

supermarket
el supermercado

cyclist
el (la) ciclista

gas station
**la estación de
gasolina**

lamppost
el farol

car
el coche

our house
nuestra casa

church
la iglesia

motorcycle
la motocicleta

bus
el autobús

airplane
el avión

café
la cafetería

statue
la estatua

station
la estación

train
el tren

canal
el canal

fire engine
el camión de bomberos

street
la calle

apartments
los departamentos

sidewalk
la acera

hotel
el hotel

telephone booth
caseta de teléfono

movie theater
el cine

twenty-three
veintitrés

23

tractor
el tractor

plow
el arado

henhouse
el gallinero

squirrel
una ardilla

The country
El campo

windmill
un molino

sky
el cielo

town
el pueblo

piglet
un cerdito

horse
un caballo

gate
la reja

barnyard
el corral

butterfly
una mariposa

goat
una cabra

bull
el toro

stable
el establo

hen
la gallina

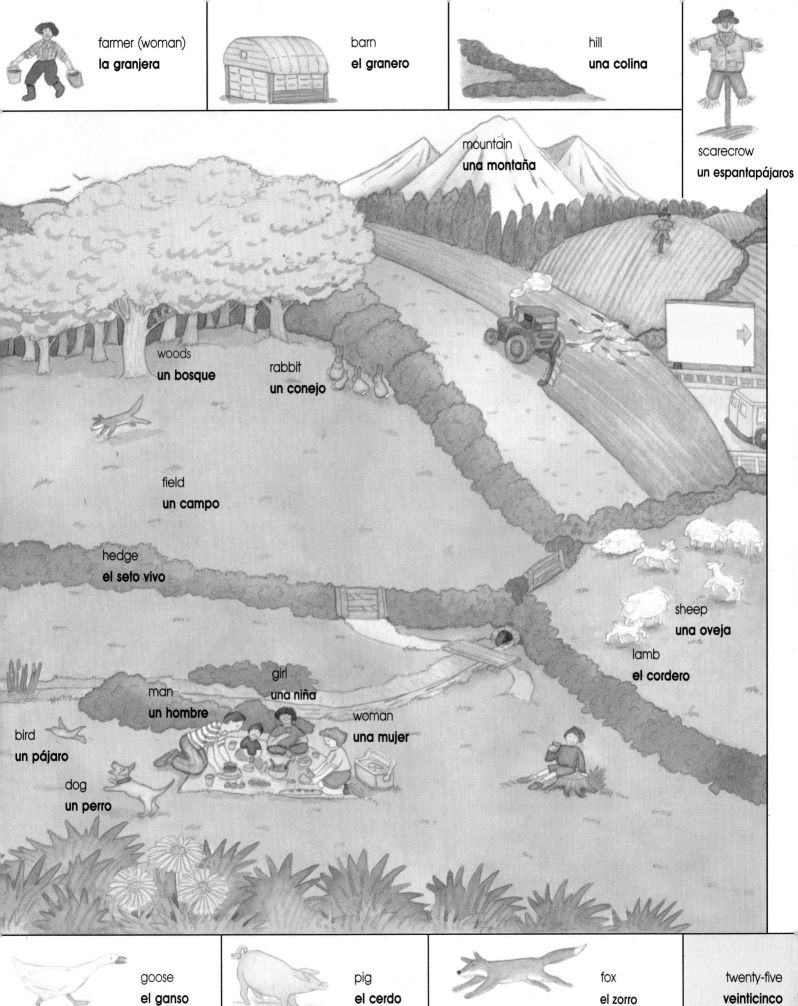

farmer (woman)
la granjera

barn
el granero

hill
una colina

scarecrow
un espantapájaros

mountain
una montaña

woods
un bosque

rabbit
un conejo

field
un campo

hedge
el seto vivo

sheep
una oveja

lamb
el cordero

girl
una niña

man
un hombre

woman
una mujer

bird
un pájaro

dog
un perro

goose
el ganso

pig
el cerdo

fox
el zorro

twenty-five
veinticinco

25

ship
un barco

sea
el mar

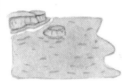
beach ball
la pelota

cabana
una cabaña

cliff
el acantilado

crab
el cangrejo

surfer
un súrfer

yacht
el yate

umbrella
la sombrilla

At the beach
En la playa

sky
el cielo

cloud
la nube

island
una isla

surfboard
la tabla de surf

motorboat
la lancha de motor

fisherman
un pescador

rowboat
la lancha de remo

seagull
la gaviota

deck chair
la tumbona

lifeguard
el salvavidas

shovel
la pala

rock
la roca

life preserver
un salvavidas

wave
la ola

cave
una cueva

shell
la concha

pail
la cubeta

seaweed
el alga (f)

ice cream
un helado

sandcastle
**un castillo
de arena**

sail
la vela

lighthouse
un faro

sand
la arena

flag
la bandera

snack bar
un puesto de refrescos

railing
la verja

climb
trepar

talk
hablar

break
romper

hang
colgar

follow
seguir

What shall we do?
¿Qué vamos a hacer?

look for
buscar

open
abrir

run
correr

push
empujar

cry
llorar

hide
esconderse

hit
pegar

hold
sostener

tear
rasgar

read
leer

smile
sonreir

think
pensar

write
escribir

jump rope
saltar la cuerda

watch
mirar

carry
cargar

sit
sentarse

pick up
levantar

pour
servir

stand
pararse

drop
dejar caer

kick
patear

shout
gritar

pull
jalar

eat
comer

drink
tomar

listen
escuchar

lean
apoyarse

play
jugar

sleep
dormir

throw
aventar

jump
saltar

catch
atrapar

point
apuntar

easel
el caballete

castle
el castillo

patient
el(la) paciente

palette
la paleta

saucepan
la cacerola

goal
la portería

microphone
el micrófono

brother and sister
un hermano y una hermana

paintbrush
el pincel

stethoscope
el estetoscopio

I want to be . . .
Quiero ser . . .

singer
un cantante / una cantante

car
un vagón

band
un conjunto

artist
un artista / una artista

engineer
el conductor

jockey
un jockey

father
el padre

mother
la madre

baby
el bebé

pillow
la almohada

child/children
el niño/los niños

soccer player
un futbolista

doctor
el doctor/la doctora

stage
el escenario

bandage
la venda

paints
las pinturas

bowl
el tazón

student
el alumno/ la alumna

computer
la computadora

drums
la batería

wastepaper basket
la papelera

actress
una actriz

pilot
el piloto

storekeeper
el tendero/la tendera

riding helmet
el casco de montar

editor
un redactor/una redactora

clown
un payaso

blackboard
un pizarrón

teacher
el maestro/la maestra

guitar
la guitarra

construction worker
un albañil

cook
una cocinera

customer
el/la cliente

reins
las riendas

saddle
la silla de montar

hard hat
un casco

brick
un ladrillo

mixer
la batidora

thirty-one
treinta y uno

31

baby
el bebé

box
la caja

lamp
la lámpara

Opposites
Los contrarios

penguin
el pingüino

bottle
la botella

skyscraper
el rascacielos

long
largo(a)

short
corto(a)

hot
caliente

cold
frío/fría

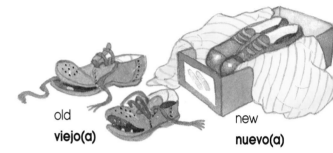
old
viejo(a)

new
nuevo(a)

wet
mojado(a)

dry
seco(a)

deep
profundo(a)

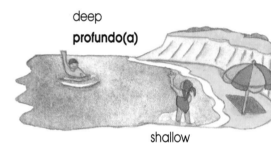
shallow
poco profundo(a)

fat
gordo(a)

thin
delgado(a)

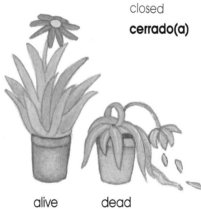
alive
vivo(a)

dead
muerto(a)

closed
cerrado(a)

open
abierto(a)

low
bajo(a)

high
alto(a)

cottage
la casita de campo

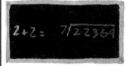
blackboard
el pizarrón

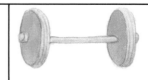
barbell
la pesa

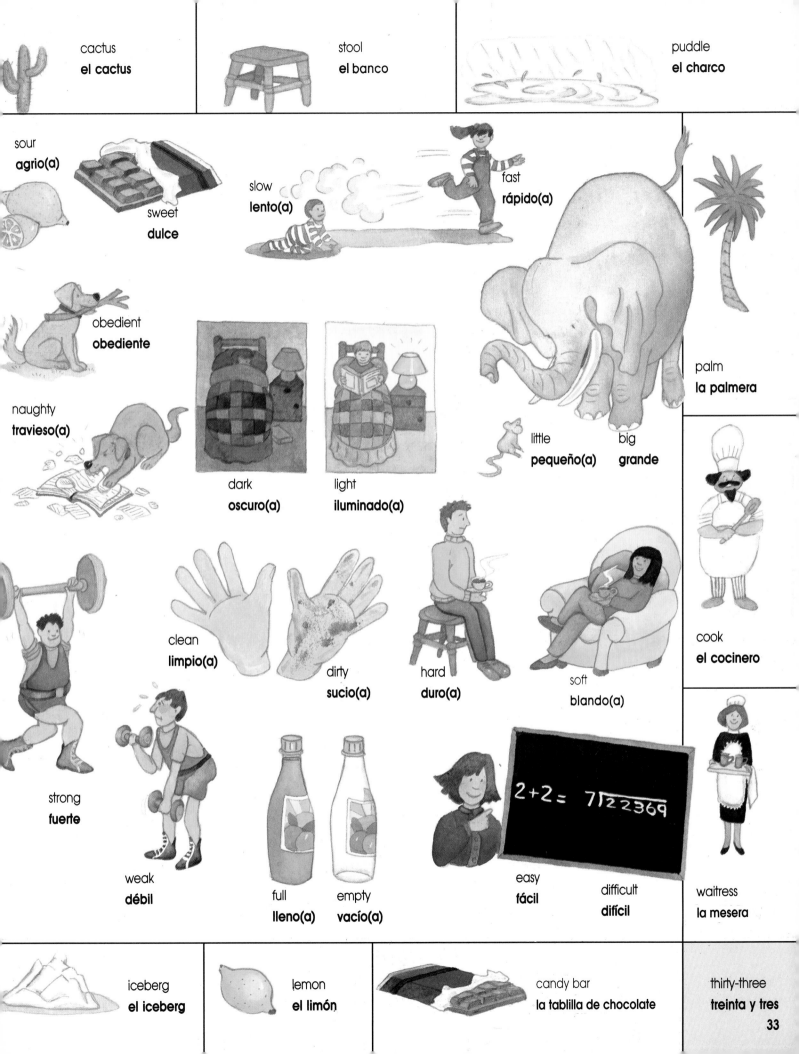

cactus
el cactus

stool
el banco

puddle
el charco

sour
agrio(a)

sweet
dulce

slow
lento(a)

fast
rápido(a)

palm
la palmera

obedient
obediente

naughty
travieso(a)

dark
oscuro(a)

light
iluminado(a)

little
pequeño(a)

big
grande

cook
el cocinero

clean
limpio(a)

dirty
sucio(a)

hard
duro(a)

soft
blando(a)

strong
fuerte

weak
débil

full
lleno(a)

empty
vacío(a)

easy
fácil

difficult
difícil

waitress
la mesera

iceberg
el iceberg

lemon
el limón

candy bar
la tablilla de chocolate

thirty-three
treinta y tres

33

I
yo

you
tu/usted
ustedes (pl)

he
el
she
ella

we
nosotros (as)

they
ellos (as)

gate
la reja

steps
los escalones

wall
el muro

Where are you?
¿Dónde estás?

From the zoo
Del zoológico

To the zoo
Al zoológico

over
por encima

under
debajo

first
primero (a)

last
último(a)

jump rope
la cuerda para saltar

behind
detrás

in front
en frente

with
con

without
sin

monkey bars
el pasamanos

sandbox
el cajón de arena

Three little words
Tres pequeñas palabras

and
y

but
pero

very
muy

up
arriba

down
abajo

far
lejos

out of
fuera de

on
encima

through
por

into
en

near
cerca

beside
al lado

outside
afuera

inside
adentro

among
entre

bench
la banca

garbage can
el basurero

signpost
el letrero

slide
la resbaladilla

tunnel
el túnel

seesaw
el subibaja

thirty-five
treinta y cinco

35

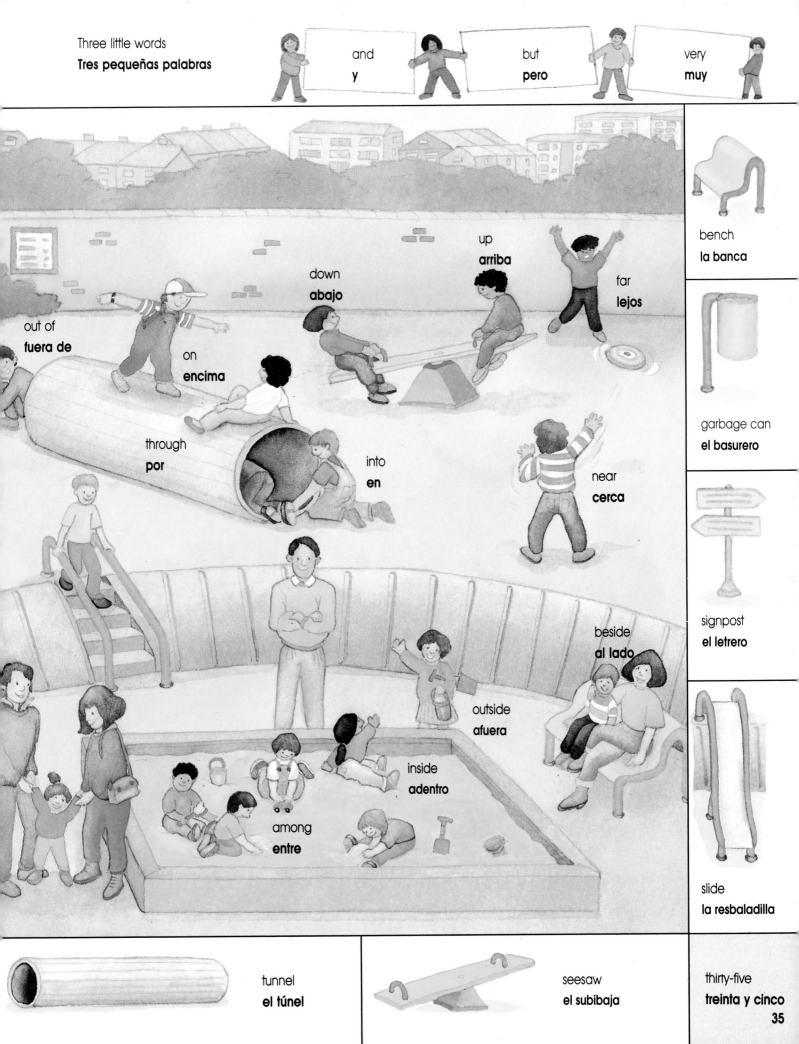

sled
un trineo

rain
la lluvia

snow
la nieve

snowman
el mono de nieve

wind
el viento

What's the weather?
¿Qué tiempo hace?

the months
los meses (m)

January	May	September
enero	**mayo**	**septiembre**
February	June	October
febrero	**junio**	**octubre**
March	July	November
marzo	**julio**	**noviembre**
April	August	December
abril	**agosto**	**diciembre**

year
un año

seasons
las estaciones

lamb
un cordero

spring
la primavera

It's a nice day.
Es un lindo día.

sun
el sol

summer
el verano

It is warm.
Hace calor.

fall
el otoño

It is windy.
Hace viento.

winter
el invierno

It is cold.
Hace frío.

daffodil
el narciso

rainbow
un arcoiris

rooster
un gallo

morning
la mañana

afternoon
la tarde

evening
la tarde

night
la noche

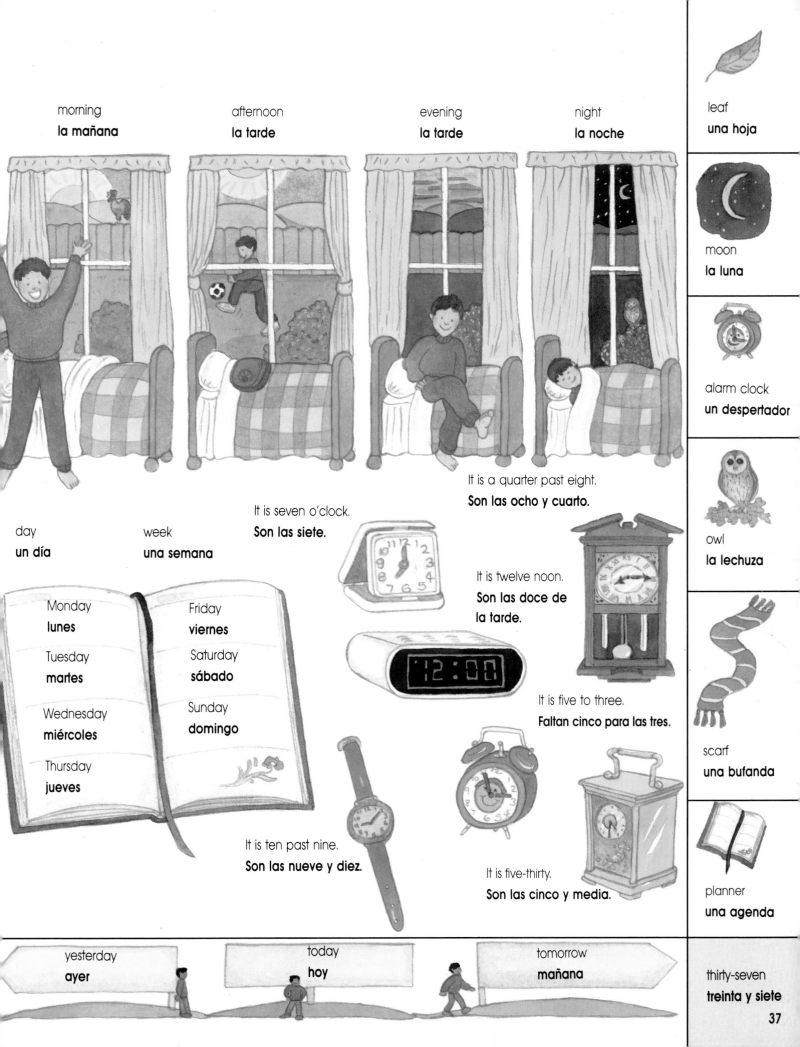

leaf
una hoja

moon
la luna

alarm clock
un despertador

owl
la lechuza

scarf
una bufanda

planner
una agenda

day
un día

week
una semana

It is seven o'clock.
Son las siete.

It is a quarter past eight.
Son las ocho y cuarto.

It is twelve noon.
Son las doce de la tarde.

It is five to three.
Faltan cinco para las tres.

Monday **lunes**	Friday **viernes**
Tuesday **martes**	Saturday **sábado**
Wednesday **miércoles**	Sunday **domingo**
Thursday **jueves**	

It is ten past nine.
Son las nueve y diez.

It is five-thirty.
Son las cinco y media.

yesterday
ayer

today
hoy

tomorrow
mañana

thirty-seven
treinta y siete

37

Where?	I have	You have	he has	she has
¿Dónde?	**yo tengo**	**tu tienes**	**el tiene**	**ella tiene**
		usted tiene		

How much?
¿Cuánto?

How many?
**¿Cuántos/
Cuántas?**

When?
¿Cuándo?

Why?
¿Por qué?

How are things?
¿Qué tal?

Do you have … ?
¿Tiene usted ….?

Is there ….?
¿Hay?

Do you speak
Spanish/English?
**¿Habla español/
inglés?**

Simple phrases
Frases sencillas

Hello. How are you?
Hola. ¿Cómo estás?

Goodbye. See you soon.
Adiós. Hasta luego.

Excuse me.
Perdón.

How old are you?
¿Cuántos años tiene? I am ninety years old.
Tengo noventa años.

Private
Privado

What's your name?
¿Cómo te llamas?

What time is it?
¿Qué horas son?
It is six o'clock.
Son las seis.

we have	you have	they have	I am	you are
nosotros tenemos	**ustedes tienen**	**ellos/ellas tienen**	**yo soy**	**tu eres** **usted es**

he is
el es

she is
ella es

Mr. Smith
Señor Martínez

Mrs. Smith
Señora Martínez

Miss Smith
Señorita Martínez

man	father	woman	mother	girl	daughter
un hombre	**el padre**	**una mujer**	**la madre**	**una niña**	**la hija**

we are
nosotros somos

you are
ustedes son

they are
ellos/ellas son

on the left	on the right	straight ahead	behind	in front of
a la izquierda	**a la derecha**	**todo derecho**	**atrás**	**en frente**

please
por favor

thank you
gracias

open	closed	I am hungry.	I am thirsty.
abierto	**cerrado**	**Tengo hambre.**	**Tengo sed.**

Word list/Vocabulario

English—Spanish

actor	un actor	child	el niño	fox	el zorro
actress	una actriz	children	los niños	freeway	una autopista
afternoon	la tarde	chimney	la chimenea	Friday	viernes
airplane	un avión	chin	la barbilla	full	lleno (a)
airport	el aeropuerto	church	la iglesia		
alarm clock	un despertador	clean	limpio (a)	garage	el garage
alive	vivo(a)	cliff	el acantilado	garbage can	el basurero
among	entre	climb	trepar	gas station	una gasolinería
and	y	clock	el reloj	gate	la reja
ankle	el tobillo	closed	cerrado (a)	gelatin	la gelatina
antenna	una antena	cloud	la nube	giraffe	la jirafa
apartments	los departamentos	clown	el payaso	girl	la niña
April	abril	coat	el abrigo	glass	el vaso
arm	el brazo	cold	frío (a)	glider	un planeador
armchair	el sillón	comb	el peine	gloves	los guantes
artist	el artista	comforter	la colchoneta	goal	la portería
astronaut	el astronauta	computer	la computadora	goat	una cabra
August	agosto	construction worker	un albañil	good-bye	adios
		control tower	la torre de control	goose	el ganso
baby	el bebé	cookie	la galleta	greenhouse	un invernadero
back	la espalda	cottage	la cabaña	guitar	la guitarra
backyard	el jardín	cracker	la sorpresa		
bag	la bolsa	cry	llorar	hair	el pelo
ballet dancer	la bailarina	curtain	la cortina	hairbrush	el cepillo para el pelo
balloon	un globo	customer	el cliente	hamburger	la hamburguesa
band	un conjunto	cyclist	el/la ciclista	hand	la mano
bandage	una venda			handkerchief	el pañuelo
barbell	la pesa	daffodil	el narciso	hang	colgar
barn	el granero	daughter	la hija	hanger	el gancho
barnyard	el corral	day	un día	hard	difícil
bat	un murciélago	dead	muerto (a)	hard	duro (a)
bathing suit	el traje de baño	December	diciembre	hat	el sombrero
bathrobe	la bata	deck chair	la tumbona	he	él
bathroom	el baño	deep	profundo (a)	head	la cabeza
bathtub	la tina	deer	un venado	hedge	el seto vivo
beach ball	una pelota	dirty	sucio (a)	helicopter	el helicóptero
beard	la barba	doctor	el doctor/la doctora	hello	hola
bed	la cama	dog	el perro	helmet	el casco
bedroom	la recámara	dog collar	el collar	hen	la gallina
bee	un abeja	dollhouse	la casita de muñecas	henhouse	el gallinero
behind	detrás	dominoes	el dominó	high	alto (a)
belt	el cinturón	donkey	un burro	hill	una colina
bench	la banca	door	la puerta	hit	pegar
beside	al lado	downtown	el centro	hold	sostener
bicycle	la bicicleta	dress	el vestido	hood	el cofre
big	grande	drink	tomar	hood	capuchón
bird	un pájaro	drinking straw	el popote	horse	un caballo
blackboard	el pizarrón	driver	el conductor	hose	la manguera
blindfold	la pañoleta	drop	dejar caer	hot	caliente
blocks	los blocs	drop (noun)	gota	hot-air balloon	un globo
book	el libro	drums	la batería	hotel	el hotel
bookbag	la mochila	dry	seco (a)	hour	la hora
bookcase	el librero	duck	un pato	house	la casa
bottle	la botella			hovercraft	un aerodeslizador
bottom	el trasero	eagle	un águila	hunger	hambre
bow	el moño	ear	la oreja		
bowl	el tazón	easel	el caballete	ice cream	un helado
box	la caja	easy	fácil	iceberg	el iceberg
boy	el niño	eat	comer	in front	en frente
break	romper	editor	un redactor	inside	adentro
bridge	el puente	eighteen-wheeler	un camión articulado	into	en
broom	una escoba	elbow	el codo	island	una isla
brother	un hermano	empty	vacío (a)		
bull	el toro	evening	la tarde	January	enero
bus	el autobús	eye	el ojo	jigsaw puzzle	el rompecabezas
but	pero			jockey	un jockey
butterfly	mariposa	face	la cara	jogger	un corredor
		factory	la fábrica	July	julio
café	la cafetería	fall	el otoño	jump	saltar
cake	el pastel	far	lejos	jump rope	saltar la cuerda
camera	la cámara	farmer	el granjero/la granjera	jump rope	la cuerda para saltar
canal	el canal	father	el padre	June	junio
candle	la vela	February	febrero		
candy bar	una tablilla de chocolate	field	un campo	kick	patear
canoe	una canoa	finger	el dedo	kitchen	la cocina
cape	la capa	fire engine	el camión de bomberos	kite	la cometa
car	el coche o automóvil	firefighter	el bombero	knee	la rodilla
car	un vagón	fish	un pez	knight	el caballero
card	la tarjeta	fisherman	un pescador		
carry	cargar	fishing rod	una caña de pescar	ladder	la escalera
castle	el castillo	flag	la bandera	lamb	el cordero
cat	el gato	flashlight	la linterna	lamp	la lámpara
catch	atrapar	floor	el suelo	lamppost	el farol
cave	una cueva	flowerbed	un macizo	lantern	la linterna
chair	la silla	follow	seguir	lawn	el césped
cheek	la mejilla	food	la comida	lawnmower	un cortacésped
chest	el pecho	foot	el pie	leaf	una hoja
				lean	apoyarse

leash	la correa
left	la izquierda
leg	la pierna
lemon	el limón
leopard	un leopardo
life preserver	un salvavidas
lifeguard	el salvavidas
light	iluminado (a)
lighthouse	un faro
lion	un león
lioness	una leona
listen	escuchar
little	pequeño
living room	la sala
locomotive	la locomotora
lollipop	la paleta
long	largo (a)
look for	buscar
low	bajo (a)
man	un hombre
March	marzo
mask	la máscara
May	mayo
microphone	el micrófono
mirror	el espejo
Miss	Señorita
mobile	el móvil
Monday	lunes
monkey	un chango
month	el mes
moon	la luna
morning	la mañana
mother	la madre
motorboat	la lancha de motor
motorcycle	la motocicleta
mountain	una montaña
mouth	la boca
movie theater	el cine
Mr.	Señor
Mrs.	Señora
music	la música
naughty	travieso (a)
near	cerca
neck	el cuello
new	nuevo (a)
night	la noche
nightgown	el camisón
nose	la nariz
November	noviembre
obedient	obediente
October	octubre
oil tanker	el barco petrolero
old	viejo (a)
on	encima
open	abierto (a)
open (verb)	abrir
out of	fuera de
outside	afuera
over	por encima
owl	la lechuza o el buho
paddle	un remo
pail	la cubeta
paint	la pintura
paintbrush	el pincel
pajamas	piyamas
palette	la paleta
palm tree	la palmera
pants	los pantalones
paper hat	sombrero de papel
parrot	un perico
path	el camino
patient	el/la paciente
piano	el piano
pick up	levantar
picture	un cuadro
pig	el cerdo
pillow	la almohada
pilot	el piloto
pitchfork	la horca
planner	una agenda
plant	la planta
plate	el plato
play	jugar
please	por favor
plow	el arado
pocket	el bolsillo
pony	el poney
potato chips	las papitas fritas
pour	servir

present	el regalo
private	privado
puddle	el charco
pull	jalar
puppet	el títere
puppy	el cachorro
push	empujar
rabbit	un conejo
radio	el radio
railroad track	la vía del tren
rain	la lluvia
rainbow	un arcoiris
raincoat	un impermeable
read	leer
record	el disco
record player	el tocadiscos
reins	las riendas
riding helmet	el casco de montar
right	la derecha
river	un río
rock	la roca
roller skates	los patines de ruedas
roof	el techo
rooster	el gallo
rowboat	la lancha de remo
rubber boots	las botas de hule
rug	el tapete
run	correr
saddle	la silla de montar
sail	la vela
sailor	el marinero
sand	la arena
sandbox	el cajón de arena
sandcastle	un castillo de arena
sandwich	el sandwich
Saturday	sábado
saucepan	la cacerola
scarecrow	un espantapájaros
scarf	la bufanda
sea	el mar
seagull	la gaviota
seasons	las estaciones
seaweed	el alga
seesaw	el subibaja
September	septiembre
shallow	poco profundo (a)
she	ella
sheep	una oveja
shelf	el estante
shell	la concha
ship	un barco
shirt	la camisa
shoe	el zapato
short	corto (a)
shoulder	el hombro
shout	gritar
shovel	la pala
shower	la regadera
sidewalk	la acera
signpost	el letrero
singer	un/una cantante
sink	el lavabo
sister	una hermana
sit	sentarse
skirt	la falda
sky	el cielo
skyscraper	el rascacielos
sleep	dormir
slide	la resbaladilla
slippers	las pantuflas
slow	lento (a)
smile	sonreir
smile (noun)	sonrisa
snake	una serpiente
snow	la nieve
snowman	el mono de nieve
soccer ball	el balón
socks	los calcetines
sofa	el sofá
soft	blando (a)
soldier	el soldado
sour	agrio (a)
spider	una araña
spoon	la cuchara
spring	la primavera
squirrel	una ardilla
stable	el establo
stage	el escenario
staircase	las escaleras
stand	pararse
station	la estación

statue	la estatua
steering wheel	el volante
stethoscope	el estetoscopio
stomach	el estómago
stool	el banco
storekeeper	el tendero/la tendera
stove	la estufa
straight ahead	todo derecho
street	la calle
summer	el verano
sun	el sol
Sunday	domingo
supermarket	el supermercado
surfboard	la tabla de surf
sweater	suéter
sweet	dulce
swimming pool	la piscina
swing	el columpio
table	la mesa
tail	la cola
talk	hablar
teacher	el maestro/la maestra
tear	rasgar
teddy bear	el osito de peluche
teeth	los dientes
telephone booth	la caseta de teléfono
television	la televisión
tent	una tienda de campaña
thank you	gracias
they	ellos (as)
think	pensar
thirst	sed
through	por o a través
throw	aventar
thumb	el pulgar
Thursday	jueves
tie	la corbata
tiger	un tigre
tights	las mallas
tire	una llanta
today	hoy
toe	el dedo del pie
toilet	el excusado
tomorrow	mañana
tongue	la lengua
town	el pueblo
toy chest	la caja de juguetes
tractor	el tractor
traffic	el tráfico
trailer	un trailer
train	el tren
tree	el árbol
tricycle	el triciclo
trowel	una paleta
truck	el camión
trunk	el tronco
Tuesday	martes
tunnel	el túnel
turtle	una tortuga
umbrella	el paraguas
umbrella (sun)	la sombrilla
under	debajo
up	árriba
van	una camioneta
very	muy
waitress	la mesera
wall	el muro/la pared (inside)
wardrobe	el ropero
warm	caliente
wastepaper basket	la papelera
watch	mirar
wave	la ola
we	nosotros (as)
Wednesday	miércoles
week	una semana
wet	mojado (a)
wheel	una rueda
wheelbarrow	una carretilla
when?	¿cuándo?
where?	¿dónde?
whistle	el silbato
why?	¿por qué?
wife	la esposa
wind	el viento
windmill	un molino
window	la ventana
windshield	el parabrisas
winter	el invierno
with	con

without	sin
wolf	un lobo
woman	una mujer
woods	un bosque
word	una palabra
write	escribir
year	un año
yesterday	ayer
zebra	la cebra

Español—Inglés

una abeja	bee
abierto (a)	open
el abrigo	coat
abril	April
abrir	open
el acantilado	cliff
la acera	sidewalk
un actor	actor
una actriz	actress
adentro	inside
adios	good-bye
un aerodeslizador	hovercraft
el aeropuerto	airport
afuera	outside
una agenda	planner
agosto	August
agrio (a)	sour
un águila	eagle
un albañil	construction worker
al lado	beside
el alga	seaweed
la almohada	pillow
alto (a)	high
el alumno/la alumna	student
un año	year
una antena	antenna
apoyarse	lean
el arado	plow
una araña	spider
el árbol	tree
el arbusto	bush
un arcoiris	rainbow
una ardilla	squirrel
la arena	sand
arriba	up
el (la) artista	artist
el astronauta	astronaut
atrapar	catch
el autobús	bus
una autopista	freeway
aventar	throw
el avión	airplane
ayer	yesterday
la bailarina	ballet dancer
bajo (a)	low
el balón de futbol	soccer ball
la banca	bench
el banco	stool
la bandera	flag
el baño	bathroom
la barba	beard
la barbilla	chin
un barco	ship
la bata	bathrobe
la batería	drums
la batidora	mixer
el bebé	baby
la bicicleta	bicycle
blando (a)	soft
la boca	mouth
la bolsa	bag
el bombero	firefighter
un bosque	woods
las botas de hule	rubber boots
la botella	bottle
el brazo	arm
una bufanda	scarf
un burro	donkey
buscar	look for
el caballero	knight
el caballete	easel
la cabeza	head
un caballo	horse
una cabra	goat
la cacerola	saucepan
el cachorro	puppy
la cafetería	café

la caja	box
la caja de juguetes	toy chest
el cajón de arena	sandbox
los calcetines	socks
caliente	warm
la calle	street
los calzoncillos	underpants
la cama	bed
la cámara	camera
el camino	path
el camión	truck
el camión de bomberos	fire engine
la camisa	shirt
el camisón	nightgown
la camiseta	undershirt
un campo	field
el canal	canal
una canoa	canoe
un/una cantante	singer
la caña de pescar	fishing rod
la capa	cape
el capuchón	hood
la cara	face
cargar	carry
una carretilla	wheelbarrow
la casa	house
la casita de muñecas	dollhouse
el casco	helmet
el casco de montar	riding helmet
la caseta de teléfono	telephone booth
el castillo	castle
un castillo de arena	sandcastle
la cebra	zebra
el cepillo para el pelo	hairbrush
cerca	near
el cerdo	pig
cerrado (a)	closed
el césped	lawn
un chango	monkey
el charco	puddle
la chimenea	chimney
el cielo	sky
el cine	movie theater
el cinturón	belt
el cliente	customer
el coche	car
una cocinera/ un cocinero	cook
la cocina	kitchen
el codo	elbow
el cofre	hood
la cola	tail
la colchoneta	comforter
colgar	hang
una colina	hill
el columpio	swing
comer	eat
la cometa	kite
la comida	food
la computadora	computer
con	with
la concha	shell
el conductor	driver
un conejo	rabbit
un conjunto	band
la corbata	tie
una corbata de moño	bow tie
un cordero	lamb
el corral	barnyard
correa	leash
un corredor	jogger
correr	run
un cortacésped	lawnmower
la cortina	curtain
corto (a)	short
un cuadro	picture
¿cuándo?	when?
la cubeta	pail
la cuchara	spoon
el cuello	neck
la cuerda para saltar	jump rope
una cueva	cave
debajo	under
el dedo	finger
el dedo del pie	toe
dejar caer	drop
un delfín	dolphin
los departamentos	apartments
la derecha	right
un despertador	alarm clock
detrás	behind
un día	day

diciembre	December
los dientes	teeth
difícil	hard
el disco	record
el doctor/la doctora	doctor
el dominó	dominoes
domingo	Sunday
¿dónde?	where?
dormir	sleep
dulce	sweet
duro (a)	hard
él	he
ella	she
ellos (as)	they
en	into
enero	January
en frente	in front
entre	among
una escalera	ladder
las escaleras	staircase
los escalones	steps
el escenario	stage
una escoba	broom
esconderse	hide
escribir	write
escuchar	listen
la espalda	back
un espantapájaros	scarecrow
el espejo	mirror
la esposa	wife
el establo	stable
la estación	station
las estaciones	seasons
el estante	shelf
la estatua	statue
el estetoscopio	stethoscope
el estómago	stomach
la estufa	stove
el excusado	toilet
la fábrica	factory
fácil	easy
la falda	skirt
un faro	lighthouse
el farol	lamppost
febrero	February
frío (a)	cold
fuera	out of
un futbolista	soccer player
la galleta	cookie
la gallina	hen
el gallinero	henhouse
un gallo	rooster
el gancho	hanger
el ganso	goose
el garage	garage
la gasolinería	gas station
el gato	cat
la gaviota	seagull
la gelatina	gelatin
gracias	thank you
grande	big
la granjera/el granjero	farmer
gritar	shout
los guantes	gloves
la guitarra	guitar
hablar	talk
hambre	hunger
la hamburguesa	hamburger
un helado	ice cream
el helicóptero	helicopter
un hermano	brother
una hermana	sister
la hija	daughter
una hoja	leaf
hola	hello
un hombre	man
el hombro	shoulder
la hora	hour
la horca	pitchfork
el hotel	hotel
hoy	today
el iceberg	iceberg
la iglesia	church
iluminado (a)	light
el impermeable	raincoat
un invernadero	greenhouse
el invierno	winter
una isla	island
la izquierda	left

el jardín	backyard
jalar	pull
una jirafa	giraffe
un jockey	jockey
jueves	Thursday
jugar	play
julio	July
junio	June
un ladrillo	brick
la lámpara	lamp
la lancha de motor	motorboat
la lancha de remo	rowboat
largo (a)	long
el lavabo	sink
la lechuza	owl
leer	read
lejos	far
la lengua	tongue
lento (a)	slow
un león	lion
una leona	lioness
un leopardo	leopard
el letrero	signpost
levantar	pick up
el librero	bookcase
el libro	book
el limón	lemon
limpio (a)	clean
la linterna	lantern/flashlight
una llanta	tire
lleno (a)	full
llorar	cry
la lluvia	rain
un lobo	wolf
la locomotora	locomotive
la luna	moon
lunes	Monday
una maceta	flowerpot
la madre	mother
el maestro/la maestra	teacher
las mallas	tights
la manguera	hose
la mano	hand
mañana	tomorrow
la mañana	morning
el mar	sea
el marinero	sailor
una mariposa	butterfly
martes	Tuesday
marzo	March
la máscara	mask
mayo	May
la mejilla	cheek
el mes	month
la mesa	table
la mesera	waitress
el micrófono	microphone
miércoles	Wednesday
mirar	watch
la mochila	bookbag or backpack
mojado (a)	wet
un molino	windmill
el mono de nieve	snowman
una montaña	mountain
la motocicleta	motorcycle
el móvil	mobile
muerto (a)	dead
una mujer	woman
un murciélago	bat
el muro	wall
la música	music
muy	very
el narciso	daffodil
la nariz	nose
la nieve	snow
la niña	girl
el niño	boy
los niños	children
la noche	night
nosotros (as)	we
noviembre	November
la nube	cloud
nuevo (a)	new
obediente	obedient
octubre	October
el ojo	eye
el bolsillo	pocket
la ola	wave
la oreja	ear
oscuro (a)	dark
el osito de peluche	teddy bear
el otoño	fall
una oveja	sheep
el/la paciente	patient
el padre	father
la pala	shovel
una palabra	word
la paleta	palette/lollipop
la palma	palm tree
los pantalones	pants
las pantuflas	slippers
el pañuelo	handkerchief
la papelera	wastepaper basket
el parabrisas	windshield
el paraguas	umbrella
la pared	wall
un pájaro	bird
las papitas fritas	potato chips
el pastel	cake
los patines de ruedas	roller skates
un pato	duck
el payaso	clown
el pecho	chest
pegar	hit
el peine	comb
un pelícano	pelican
el pelo	hair
la pelota	beach ball
pensar	think
pequeño (a)	little
un perico	parrot
pero	but
un perro	dog
la pesa	barbell
un pescador	fisherman
un pez	fish
el piano	piano
el pie	foot
la pierna	leg
el piloto	pilot
el pincel	paintbrush
las pinturas	paints
la piscina	swimming pool
las piyamas	pajamas
el pizarrón	blackboard
un planeador	glider
la planta	plant
el plato	plate
poco profundo (a)	shallow
el poney	pony
el popote	drinking straw
por	through
por encima	over
por favor	please
¿por qué?	why?
la portería	goal
la primavera	spring
primero (a)	first
privado	private
profundo (a)	deep
el pueblo	town
el puente	bridge
la puerta	door
el pulgar	thumb
el radio	radio
rápido (a)	fast
el rascacielos	skyscraper
rasgar	tear
la recámara	bedroom
un redactor/una redactora	editor
la regadera	shower/watering can
el regalo	present
el reloj	clock
la reja	gate
un remo	paddle
la resbaladilla	slide
las riendas	reins
un río	river
la roca	rock
la rodilla	knee
romper	break
el rompecabezas	jigsaw puzzle
el ropero	wardrobe
una rueda	wheel
sábado	Saturday
la sala	living room
saltar la cuerda	jump rope
saltar	jump
un salvavidas	life preserver/lifeguard
el sandwich	sandwich
seco (a)	dry
sed	thirst
seguir	follow
una semana	week
sentarse	sit
Señor	Mr.
Señora	Mrs.
Señorita	Miss
septiembre	September
una serpiente	snake
servir	pour
el seto vivo	hedge
la silla	chair
la silla de montar	saddle
el sillón	armchair
sin	without
el sofá	sofa
el sol	sun
el soldado	soldier
el sombrero	hat
el sombrero de papel	paper hat
la sombrilla	umbrella (sun)
sonreir	smile
sonrisa	smile
la sorpresa	cracker
sostener	hold
el subibaja	seesaw
sucio (a)	dirty
el suelo	floor
el suéter	sweater
el supermercado	supermarket
la tabla de surf	surfboard
la tablilla de chocolate	candy bar
el tapete	rug
la tarde	afternoon/evening
la tarjeta	card
el tazón	bowl
el techo	roof
la televisión	television
el tendero/la tendera	storekeeper
el tenedor	fork
una tienda de campaña	tent
un tigre	tiger
la tina	bathtub
el títere	puppet
el tobillo	ankle
el tocadiscos	record player
todo derecho	straight ahead
tomar	drink
el toro	bull
la torre de control	control tower
una tortuga	turtle
el tractor	tractor
el tráfico	traffic
un trailer	trailer
el trasero	bottom
travieso (a)	naughty
el tren	train
trepar	climb
el triciclo	tricycle
tu	you
el túnel	tunnel
último (a)	last
usted	you
ustedes	you (pl)
vacío (a)	empty
un vagón	car
la vaquera	cowgirl
el vaquero	cowboy
el vaso	glass
la vela	sail/candle
un venado	deer
la venda	bandage
la ventana	window
el verano	summer
el vestido	dress
la vía del tren	railroad track
viejo (a)	old
el viento	wind
viernes	Friday
vivo (a)	alive
el volante	steering wheel
y	and
yo	I
el zapato	shoe
el zorro	fox

pink
rosa

black
negro

purple
morado

red
rojo

blue
azul

yellow
amarillo

green
verde

brown
marrón

Colors and numbers
Colores y números

Newmarket Public Library

1	one **uno**	**11**	eleven **once**
2	two **dos**	**12**	twelve **doce**
3	three **tres**	**13**	thirteen **trece**
4	four **cuatro**	**14**	fourteen **catorce**
5	five **cinco**	**15**	fifteen **quince**
6	six **seis**	**16**	sixteen **dieciséis**
7	seven **siete**	**17**	seventeen **diecisiete**
8	eight **ocho**	**18**	eighteen **dieciocho**
9	nine **nueve**	**19**	nineteen **diecinueve**
10	ten **diez**	**20**	twenty **veinte**

30 thirty **treinta**

40 forty **cuarenta**

50 fifty **cincuenta**

100 one hundred **cien**

1,000 one thousand **mil**

1,000,000 one million **un millón**

44